MW01536902

This Journal belongs to

ISBN 979-8-9870476-2-0

Give Thanks

Give Thanks

Give Thanks

Give Thanks

Give Thanks

Give Thanks

Give Thanks

Give Thanks

GIVE THANKS

Give Thanks

Give Thanks

Give Thanks

Give Thanks

Give Thanks

Give Thanks

Give Thanks

GIVE THANKS

Give Thanks

Give Thanks

Give Thanks

GIVE THANKS

GIVE THANKS

Give Thanks

GIVE THANKS

Give Thanks

Give Thanks

Give Thanks

Give Thanks

Give Thanks

Give Thanks

Give Thanks

Give Thanks

Give Thanks

Give Thanks

Give Thanks

Give Thanks

Give Thanks

Give Thanks

Give Thanks

Give Thanks

Give Thanks

Give Thanks

Give Thanks

Give Thanks

Give Thanks

Give Thanks

Give Thanks

Give Thanks

Give Thanks

GIVE THANKS

Give Thanks

Give Thanks

Give Thanks

Give Thanks

Give Thanks

Give Thanks

Give Thanks

Give Thanks

Give Thanks

GIVE THANKS

Give Thanks

Give Thanks

GIVE THANKS

Give Thanks

Give Thanks

Give Thanks

Give Thanks

GIVE THANKS

Give Thanks

Give Thanks

Give Thanks

GIVE THANKS

Give Thanks

Give Thanks

Give Thanks

Give Thanks

GIVE THANKS

Give Thanks

GIVE THANKS

Give Thanks

Give Thanks

Give Thanks

Give Thanks

Give Thanks

GIVE THANKS

Give Thanks

Give Thanks

Give Thanks

Give Thanks

Give Thanks

GIVE THANKS

Give Thanks

Give Thanks

Give Thanks

Give Thanks

Give Thanks

Give Thanks

Give Thanks

Made in the USA
Las Vegas, NV
13 December 2022

62124693R00056